I0760131

LYNDON B. JOHNSON

PIVOTAL PRESIDENTS

PROFILES IN LEADERSHIP

LYNDON B. JOHNSON

Edited by Meredith Day

Published in 2017 by Britannica Educational Publishing (a trademark of Encyclopædia Britannica, Inc.) in association with The Rosen Publishing Group, Inc.
29 East 21st Street, New York, NY 10010

Distributed exclusively by Rosen Publishing.
To see additional Britannica Educational Publishing titles, go to rosenpublishing.com.

First Edition

Britannica Educational Publishing
J.E. Luebering: Executive Director, Core Editorial
Anthony L. Green: Editor, Compton's by Britannica

Rosen Publishing
Meredith Day: Editor
Nelson Sá: Art Director
Ellina Litmanovich: Designer
Cindy Reiman: Photography Manager
Bruce Donnolla: Photo Researcher

Library of Congress Cataloging-in-Publication Data

Names: Day, Meredith, editor.
Title: Lyndon B. Johnson / edited by Meredith Day.
Description: First edition. | New York : Britannica Educational Publishing in association with Rosen Educational Services, 2017. | Series: Pivotal presidents: profiles in leadership | Includes bibliographical references and index. | Audience: Grades 7-12.
Identifiers: LCCN 2015050688 | ISBN 9781680485271 (library bound : alk. paper)
Subjects: LCSH: Johnson, Lyndon B. (Lyndon Baines), 1908-1973. | Presidents--United States—Biography. | United States--Politics and government--1963-1969.
Classification: LCC E847 .L964 2016 | DDC 973.923092--dc23
LC record available at http://lccn.loc.gov/2015050688

Manufactured in China

Photo credits: Cover, p. 3 (portrait) George F. Mobley/National Geographic Image Collection/Getty Images; cover, p. 3 (background) Bob Parent/Hulton Archive/Getty Images; cover, pp. 1, 3 (flag) © iStockphoto.com/spxChrome; p. 6 Lyndon B. Johnson Library Photo; pp. 13, 20, 51 Everett Collection Historical/Alamy; p. 14 Hank Walker/The LIFE Picture Collection/Getty Images; pp. 16, 25, 30, 32, 35, 37, 43, 57, 64 ©AP Images; p. 23 Fotosearch/Archive Photos/Getty Images; pp. 28, 68 NASA; p. 41 Michael Rougier/The LIFE Picture Collection/Getty Images; p. 45 Hulton Archive/Archive Photos/Getty Images; p. 48 Encyclopædia Britannica, Inc.; p. 53 MPI/Archive Photos/Getty Images; p. 54 Douglas Graham/CQ Roll Call Group/Getty Images; p. 61 Anthony Barboza/Archive Photos/Getty Images; p. 62 Three Lions/Hulton Archive/Getty Images; p. 66 Francis Miller/The LIFE Picture Collection/Getty Images; interior pages flag Fedorov Oleksiy/Shutterstock.com.

Table of Contents

Introduction

Jacqueline Kennedy *(right)* and Lady Bird Johnson stand by Lyndon B. Johnson as he takes the oath of office aboard Air Force One after the assassination of President John F. Kennedy on November 22, 1963.

At 2:38 PM, on November 22, 1963, Lyndon B. Johnson took the oath of office as the 36th president of the United States. On his right stood his wife, Lady Bird. On his left stood Jacqueline Kennedy, stony-faced with shock. Less than two hours earlier, President John F. Kennedy had died in a Dallas hospital from an assassin's bullets. He had been shot while riding in a motorcade through downtown Dallas. Johnson, riding two cars behind Kennedy, was unhurt.

As vice president of the United States, Lyndon Johnson immediately became president. He was the fourth vice president to be thrust into the nation's top office by the assassination of his predecessor. The new president's first message to the nation, televised the evening of that fateful day on his arrival at Andrews Air Force Base, near Washington, D.C., was brief. "I will do my best. That is all I can do. I ask for your help, and God's."

Johnson immediately went to work passing legislation that had been proposed by the Kennedy Administration. Having been the Senate majority leader before his election as vice president, he was skilled at negotiating with congressmen to achieve desired results. The Civil Rights Act of 1964 was the most important of these measures passed in his first year as president. Johnson, as a Texan, may have seemed to be an unlikely champion of civil rights, given that the Southern states were the most likely to institutionalize racial discrimination. However, as a young man, Johnson had taught impoverished Mexican American children, and this experience partly inspired his commitment to antipoverty and civil rights programs.

On November 3, 1964, the voters of the nation elected Johnson to a full term. He overwhelmingly defeated Republican Senator Barry M. Goldwater of Arizona. Johnson called his landslide victory "a tribute to the program that was begun by our beloved president, John F. Kennedy."

Johnson referred to his administration's programs as the Great Society, by which he aimed to improve life for Americans of all races and economic backgrounds. Other landmark legislation enacted during his presidency included the Voting Rights Act, the Immigration and Nationality Act, and an amendment to the Social Security Act that established

Medicare and Medicaid. Unfortunately, the Vietnam War would eventually overshadow his domestic agenda.

After the bombing of a U.S. ship in the Gulf of Tonkin in 1964, Johnson greatly expanded the U.S. role in Vietnam. However, the North Vietnamese found success with their guerrilla tactics. Johnson sent more troops in hopes of turning the tide of the war, but this escalation was extremely costly—not only in dollars, but also in American lives and public support. As antiwar protests grew, so did dissatisfaction among poor African Americans who felt that the promises of the Great Society had gone unfulfilled. Beginning in the mid-1960s, race riots erupted in cities across the country.

On March 31, 1968, the embattled president made a shocking announcement: he would not run for reelection in November. Under the Twenty-second Amendment of the U.S. Constitution, he was eligible to run for a second full term because he had served out fewer than two years of Kennedy's term. But the challenges both at home and abroad convinced Johnson that the country needed new leadership. In the same speech, he announced that bombing in North Vietnam would be reduced and that he would seek to begin negotiations to end the war.

Johnson's presidency, begun in tragedy, thus came to an unexpected conclusion. Nevertheless, his administration had led the way on social-welfare reform. Though the war in Vietnam prevented him from reaching the full potential of his program, Johnson's legacy as a champion of civil rights and the rights of ordinary Americans lives on.

CHAPTER 1

Early Life and Career

Lyndon B. Johnson, a six-foot-three-inch Texan, had an air of the frontier even when he was not wearing his ten-gallon hat. Visitors to his LBJ Ranch, near Johnson City, were shown two stone forts built by his grandfather, Samuel Ealy Johnson, founder of Johnson City. They were constructed to protect the first settlers from Indian raids.

His grandfather served in the Texas state legislature and became Texas secretary of state. Legend has it that when he first saw the infant Lyndon, he is said to have prophesied that his grandson would someday be a United States senator.

A Son of Texas Pioneers

Lyndon Baines Johnson was born on August 27, 1908, on a farm near Stonewall, in the hills of south-central Texas. He was the eldest of five children, including three sisters and a brother, Sam Houston Johnson.

Johnson's father, Samuel Ealy Johnson, Jr., at his desk in the Texas state capitol

Johnson's father, Samuel Ealy Johnson, Jr., was a farmer and schoolteacher. He too was a member of the state legislature, where he was a colleague and close friend of Sam Rayburn, a fellow Democrat who later became Speaker of the U.S. House of Representatives and served there for more than 48 years. Samuel Johnson had earlier lost money in cotton speculation, and, despite his legislative career, the family often struggled to make a living.

Johnson and Sam Rayburn in 1954, when Johnson was a senator and Rayburn was Speaker of the House.

Johnson's mother was Rebekah Baines Johnson. Her family also had been pioneers of central Texas. Her grandfather was the Reverend George W. Baines (the name was originally spelled Bains). He was a Baptist leader in Texas during the American Civil War and was president of Baylor University for two years (1861–63). Rebekah's father, Joseph W. Baines, was a representative in the state legislature. Her mother was a niece of a member of the first Congress of the Republic of Texas. Her forebears for generations had represented their home district in the Scottish Parliament. Rebekah Baines was a graduate of Baylor University and taught school before her marriage.

When Lyndon was five, the family moved to Johnson City. To help earn his way, young Lyndon shined shoes in the "city's" only barber shop and herded goats for the ranchers.

Education and Teaching

Lyndon finished high school in 1924, at the age of only 15, and with a group of friends worked his way on freight trains to California. Odd jobs provided scarcely enough food for the rapidly growing, lanky youth. Hungry and homesick, he hitchhiked back to Johnson City and took a job on a road-building gang. By this time he began to realize that his parents were right in insisting on a college education. "It became increasingly apparent to me," he said later, "that there was something to this idea of higher education."

With a little borrowed money he set out for Southwest Texas State Teachers College, in San Marcos, in 1927. He paid his expenses with part-time jobs as janitor, secretary to the college president, and door-to-door hosiery

Johnson *(back row, center)* **with the Athletic Club at Welhausen Elementary School in 1928**

salesman. Forced to quit school temporarily when his money ran out, he taught Mexican American children in the small southern Texas town of Cotulla. The extreme poverty of his students made a profound impression on him.

Return to Cotulla

Johnson's time as a teacher, though brief, inspired much of his mission to expand educational opportunities and eliminate poverty as president. On November 7, 1966, he returned to Cotulla, Texas, to give a speech at the Welhausen Elementary School where he had taught 38 years earlier. He noted that while the school had better programs than it had when he was there, much progress still remained to be made. For example, Mexican American students in districts such as Cotulla dropped out of school at a much higher rate than white students. The president called education "our greatest national resource" and declared:

> *No longer can we afford to say to one group of children: Your goal should be to climb as high as you can. And then say to another group: Your goal should be to get out as soon as you can. ... The citizenship of America today looks forward to the time in the near future when every boy and girl born in this country will have the right*

continued on the next page

continued from the previous page

and the opportunity to get all the education that they can take. And when they have that right, when they have that opportunity, from Head Start to a college Ph.D. degree, a great many of them will exercise it—they will profit from it—we will have a better and a stronger, and, what is very important, a more prosperous and happier America.

A year later he was able to repay the money he had borrowed. He bought some athletic equipment for the underprivileged children of the town and took one small boy back home with him for private instruction by his mother. Through his later work in state politics, Johnson developed close and enduring ties to the Mexican American community in Texas—a factor that would help the Kennedy-Johnson ticket carry Texas in the presidential election of 1960.

Johnson returned to the teachers college and got his degree in 1930. He then taught public speaking and debate at a Houston high school for two years.

Politics and Marriage

Johnson entered politics at the age of 24, when Congressman Richard M. Kleberg, one of the owners of the famous King Ranch, took him to Washington, D.C., as his secretary (1932–35). His political ability was recognized even then. He worked tirelessly on behalf of Kleberg's constituents and quickly developed a thorough grasp of congressional politics. He was elected speaker of the "Little Congress," an organization of congressional secretaries.

In 1934 Johnson met Claudia Alta Taylor, daughter of a wealthy Marshall, Texas, rancher. He knew immediately that she was the woman he wanted to marry. They were married on November 17, 1934. When Claudia was a baby, she was nicknamed Lady Bird by a family servant who declared she was "purty as a ladybird." From then on she was never called by any other name. The Johnsons had two daughters—Lynda Bird, born in 1944, and Luci Baines, born in 1947.

A recent graduate of the University of Texas, where she finished near the top of

Lyndon and Lady Bird Johnson with their daughters, Lynda Bird and Luci Baines, in 1948

her class, Lady Bird Johnson was a much-needed source of stability in her husband's life as well as a shrewd judge of people. She was an astute businesswoman who built up the family fortune while her husband occupied himself in public office. With an inheritance from her parents, she bought a radio station in Austin that was losing money. Eventually the LBJ Company, Inc., came to control several radio-television stations, a bank, large real-estate holdings, and other valuable properties. When Johnson became vice president in 1960, he and Mrs. Johnson transferred the control of this company to trustees.

CHAPTER 2

Congress and Vice Presidency

Sam Rayburn, the old family friend, got Johnson his first important public job, as Texas director of the National Youth Administration (NYA). The NYA, part of the Works Progress Administration, helped young men and women between the ages of 16 and 25 complete their education by providing part-time jobs for students. Jobs and training in various fields also helped reduce unemployment among young people.

Two years later Johnson, a Democrat, was elected to the U.S. House of Representatives to fill a vacancy left by the death of James P. Buchanan. His victory on an all-out New Deal platform attracted the attention of President Franklin D. Roosevelt, who was vacationing in Texas at the time. Roosevelt asked the new congressman to return to Washington with him on the presidential train. He then became identified as one of the "Young Guard" of Roosevelt supporters.

The day following the Japanese attack on Pearl Harbor in December 1941, Johnson became the first member of Congress to

Johnson in New Guinea during his stint as an officer in the U.S. Navy during World War II

enter active duty in World War II. A lieutenant commander in the Navy, he was stationed in New Zealand and Australia. While he was overseas, his wife, Lady Bird, ran his congressional office. In July 1942 President Roosevelt ordered all congressmen in the armed forces to return to Congress, ending Johnson's tour of duty.

Senator and Party Leader

Johnson served five successive full terms in the House. Among the causes he championed were the creation of federal public housing and the expansion of electricity to isolated rural areas. During one year of this time he also studied at the Georgetown University Law School. He ran unsuccessfully for a seat in the U.S. Senate in a special election in 1941. Running again in 1948, he won the Democratic primary (which in Texas was tantamount to election) after a vicious campaign that included voter fraud on both sides. His extraordinarily slim margin of victory—87 votes out of 988,000 votes cast—earned him the ironic nickname "Landslide Lyndon."

Senate Majority Leader Johnson *(far right)* in 1957 with fellow Democratic senators, including future president John F. Kennedy *(far left)* and Johnson's future vice president, Hubert H. Humphrey *(center)*

He remained in the Senate for 12 years, becoming Democratic whip in 1951 and minority leader in 1953. With the return of a Democratic majority in 1955, Johnson, age 46, became the youngest majority leader in that body's history. He quickly established himself as one of the most effective and persuasive party leaders in memory. The 18-hour working days he put in may have contributed to a severe heart attack—which he would later describe as "the worst a man could have and still live"—in the summer of 1955. By the next session of Congress, five months later, he was back at work.

Bipartisanship

In his first State of the Union address, President Dwight D. Eisenhower called for bipartisanship. As a centrist Republican, he often disagreed with the more conservative, anticommunist wing of his own party, which made collaboration with the Democrats even more vital. Voters also encouraged this approach, as Democrats held control of both houses of Congress for most of Eisenhower's presidency.

As Senate majority leader, Johnson earned a reputation for building coalitions between different factions of the Democratic Party, as well as collaborating with moderate Republicans. He was a master at understanding and balancing the many political factors at play within both parties. While the Eisenhower Administration focused on foreign policy, Johnson skillfully maneuvered his colleagues in the Senate to pass reform measures such as the 1955 public housing bill and the 1957 civil rights bill. Though the latter was watered down to prevent the Southern Democrats from

blocking its passage, the first civil rights act since the end of Reconstruction was still a major achievement.

The intraparty divisions of both the Republicans and the Democrats allowed for this spirit of bipartisanship in the 1950s. In subsequent decades, both parties would become more rigid in their ideologies, which limited cooperation between them.

During his years in the Senate, Johnson developed a talent for negotiating and reaching accommodation among divergent political factions. His greatest accomplishment was to obtain passage through the Senate of the first civil rights bill since 1875. This 1957 bill authorized the federal government to take legal measures to prevent a citizen from being denied voting rights. It was followed by another civil rights measure in 1960. He also supported the legislation that created the National Aeronautics and Space Administration (NASA) in 1958. His committee assignments included seats on the Senate Armed Services Committee and the Appropriations Committee. By methods sometimes tactful but often ruthless, he transformed the Senate Democrats into a remarkably disciplined and cohesive bloc.

NASA administrator T. Keith Glennan (*left*) with Johnson in 1960

At the Democratic convention in 1956, Johnson received 80 votes as a favorite-son candidate for president, meaning he had support mostly from his home state of Texas. With an eye on the presidential nomination in 1960, he attempted to cultivate his reputation among supporters as a legislative statesman.

Vice President of the United States

At the Democratic convention in 1960, Johnson lost the presidential nomination to John F. Kennedy on the first ballot, 809 votes to 409. He then surprised many both inside and outside the party when he accepted Kennedy's invitation to join the Democratic ticket as the vice presidential candidate. His vigorous campaign through the Southern states is credited with winning the 81 Southern electoral votes cast for the Democrats in the election, especially the states of Texas, North Carolina, South Carolina, and Louisiana. Johnson was reelected to the Senate at the same time he was chosen vice president. He resigned from the Senate after the November elections to take up his new duties.

Johnson, the Democratic vice presidential candidate, campaigns in Houston in 1960.

Kennedy lived up to his campaign promise to make his vice president an active partner. Johnson attended Cabinet, National Security Council, and special White House meetings. He was chairman of the President's Committee on Equal Employment Opportunity, which sought to end racial discrimination in the hiring practices of government contractors. He also headed the National Advisory Council for the Peace Corps and was chairman of the National Aeronautics and Space Council.

However, Johnson regarded most of his assignments as busy work, and he was convinced that the president was ignoring him. His legendary knowledge of Congress went largely unused, despite Kennedy's failure to push through his own legislative program. His frustration was increased by the apparent disdain with which he was regarded by some prominent members of the Kennedy Administration—including the president's brother, Attorney General Robert F. Kennedy. Johnson, in turn, envied President Kennedy's handsome appearance and his reputation for urbanity and sophisticated charm. Despite Johnson's physically imposing presence (he stood six feet three inches [nearly two meters] tall and usually weighed more than 200 pounds [more than 90 kilograms]), he suffered from deep-seated feelings of inferiority, especially compared with the Kennedys, the scions of the "Eastern establishment." As he frequently said, it was his curse to have hailed from "the wrong part of the country."

President John F. Kennedy and Vice President Johnson on the White House grounds in 1961

Johnson represented the president on goodwill missions throughout the world, explaining the administration's foreign-aid policy. As a "global politician," he showed the same persuasive charm so familiar in the Senate. Secret Service agents assigned to guard him disapproved strongly of the way he plunged into crowds to shake outstretched hands. He was determined to "meet the people," to "get the feel of the folks." In October 1962 he was awarded the Grand Cross of Merit of the Sovereign Order of Malta for his "significant humanitarian contributions," the first American to be so honored by the knights of one of the oldest Roman Catholic orders.

Chapter 3

Succession to the Presidency

In November 1963 Lyndon and Lady Bird Johnson flew to Texas with President and Mrs. Kennedy on a political trip, looking forward to the 1964 presidential campaign. The Kennedys were to have vacationed at the LBJ Ranch after the Dallas visit. But on November 22, President Kennedy was assassinated as his motorcade traveled through the city.

The Vice President Becomes President

The assassination of President Kennedy plunged Johnson into the office that he had sought three years earlier. At 2:38 PM that day,

enison Herald

AD IN DALLAS

SHOTS SHOCK DENISONIANS

RROWING NATION S JFK FAREWELL

EDY KILLED; RNOR SHOT

The Longview Daily News

The Abilene Reporter-News

NT ASSASSINATED

per's Hits nally

Officer Killed; Man Charged

KENNEDY SLAI ON DALLAS STREE

THE DALLAS TIMES HERALD

CHRISTMAS BOOK SECTION

Suspect Arrested

EXTRA

Wichita Falls Times

PRESIDENT IS KILL

SAN ANGELO STANDARD-TIMES

Lyndon Johnson New Presid As Kennedy Is Slain In Dal

Charges Filed On Oswald

Kennedy In Motor LBJ Swo

nnally

Newspaper headlines announce President Kennedy's assassination and Johnson's swearing in. Texas Governor John Connally was also seriously wounded in the attack.

Johnson took the oath of office aboard the presidential plane, Air Force One, as it stood on the tarmac at Love Field, Dallas, waiting to take Kennedy's remains back to Washington. In one afternoon Johnson had been thrust into the most difficult—and most prized—role of his long political career. One of the new president's first acts was to appoint a commission to investigate the assassination of Kennedy and the shooting of Lee Harvey Oswald, the alleged assassin, two days later. Chaired by Earl Warren, the chief justice of the United States, the Warren Commission concluded in September 1964 that there had been no conspiracy in Kennedy's death.

On the evening of November 25, after the Kennedy funeral services, Johnson held a reception in the State Department Building for the 220 government leaders who had gathered from all parts of the world to honor the late president. The Johnson family moved into the White House on December 7.

President Johnson's first address to a joint session of Congress, on November 27, emphasized the theme of continuity in the U.S. government. Invoking the memory of the martyred president, he urged the passage of Kennedy's legislative agenda, which had been stalled in congressional

Johnson gives his first address to Congress as president five days after Kennedy's assassination.

committees. He placed greatest importance on Kennedy's civil rights bill, which became the focus of his efforts during the first months of his presidency. "No memorial oration or eulogy could more eloquently honor President Kennedy's memory," he said, "than the earliest possible passage of the civil rights bill." He also asked Congress to enact a tax-cut bill and stressed economy in government spending. Regarding foreign policy, he declared that "this nation will keep its commitments from South Vietnam to West Berlin." He pledged continuation of foreign aid to Africa, Asia, and Latin America, as well as support of the United Nations.

Johnson Takes a Firm Hold

When Johnson became president, he took firm command of the government, reassuring a worried world of the continuity of U.S. policy and leadership. Addressing the United Nations General Assembly on December 17, he reaffirmed his nation's dedication to world peace and called for a "peaceful revolution" that would forever wipe out hunger, poverty, and disease.

During his first few months in office Johnson moved quickly to gain support among the nation's businessmen while maintaining his party's traditionally friendly ties with organized labor. In his State of the Union message to Congress on January 8, 1964, Johnson announced "an unconditional war on poverty," reminiscent of Franklin D. Roosevelt's New Deal. Although he proposed cutting the federal budget, this still allowed for increased spending on education, health, and manpower training to help alleviate poverty. He also called for reduced military spending in spite of the continuing military involvement in Southeast Asia. Johnson's great popularity was partly the result of the nation's continuing business upswing. Hailing it as a major stimulus to the economy, he signed a multibillion-dollar tax-cut bill on February 26.

The legislation enacted during Johnson's first year was largely based on groundwork laid by the Kennedy Administration. Whereas Kennedy had called his program the "New Frontier," Johnson referred to his program as the "Great Society," which he defined as "an end to poverty and injustice, to which we are totally committed in our time." Among the first measures signed by the new president were bills authorizing almost $3 billion for aid to education, more than $1.5 billion for public works, and more than $3 billion for foreign aid. In February he signed the document that added to the Constitution the Twenty-fourth

Amendment, banning the poll tax as a prerequisite for voting in federal elections. Poll taxes were around $1.50 (or $11.48 in 2015 dollars), which was a significant amount for many black Southerners. Some states allowed local districts to levy an additional tax or required the tax to be paid for two or three years before the person was eligible to register to vote, increasing the burden on poor Americans.

Johnson's persuasive skills were shown when he helped settle a five-year-old work-rules dispute in the railway industry. When he intervened, on April 9, 1964, union and company officials agreed to postpone a threatened strike. Johnson took part in subsequent negotiations. On April 22 he announced that a "just and fair" settlement had been reached.

Crises in Panama and Southeast Asia

The new president faced grave problems in his conduct of the nation's foreign affairs. One of them grew out of clashes between Panamanian demonstrators and U.S. troops in January 1964. More than 20 people were killed. Panama then severed diplomatic relations with the United States, demanding the revision of the 1903 Panama Canal Treaty. Johnson offered a "full and frank review" of the issues but refused to make any more definite commitment. Diplomatic ties with Panama were not restored until early April.

The Pan American Airlines building was one of a number of American-owned businesses set ablaze in anti-American riots in Panama City, Panama, in January 1964.

Relations with the Soviet Union improved somewhat, but Johnson was unable to bridge the growing gulf between U.S. and French policies. The rift was most noticeable in Southeast Asia, where France advocated the neutralization of South Vietnam. Instead, the United States was determined to help fight a growing communist insurrection in North Vietnam, fought by guerrillas known as the Viet Cong. The United States sharply boosted military aid to the South Vietnamese government.

In early August 1964, after North Vietnamese gunboats allegedly attacked U.S. destroyers in the Gulf of Tonkin near the coast of North Vietnam without provocation, Johnson ordered retaliatory bombing raids on North Vietnamese naval installations. In a televised address to the nation, he proclaimed, "We still seek no wider war." Two days later, at Johnson's request, Congress overwhelmingly passed the Gulf of Tonkin Resolution, which authorized the president to take "all necessary measures to repel any armed attack against the forces of the United States and to prevent further aggression." In effect, the measure granted Johnson the constitutional authority to conduct a war in Vietnam without a formal declaration from Congress. Although there were contradictory reports about the "engagement" in the gulf—about which side did what, if anything, and when—Johnson never discussed them with the public.

An A-1 Skyraider drops bombs on targets in North Vietnam in December 1964.

The 1964 Civil Rights Act

A major event in Johnson's first year as president was congressional passage of the most far-reaching civil rights bill in the nation's history. Backed by President Kennedy, the measure had been introduced into Congress in June 1963 in the wake of nationwide civil rights demonstrations. When Johnson assumed office, he firmly supported the bill.

The bill that passed the House of Representatives in February, thanks to revisions from civil rights leaders, was much stronger than the one that Kennedy had proposed, but Southern opponents blocked its passage in the Senate. On June 10, after a record 75-day filibuster, a bipartisan coalition voted cloture—the first time in history that the Senate had voted to cut off debate on a civil rights measure. The bill then passed the Senate, 73 to 27. On July 2 President Johnson signed the historic measure.

The Civil Rights Act of 1964 was intended to end discrimination based on race, color, religion, or national origin. Among its provisions, Title I of the act guarantees equal voting rights by removing registration requirements

Johnson shakes hands with Dr. Martin Luther King, Jr., after signing the Civil Rights Act of 1964.

and procedures biased against minorities and the underprivileged. Title II prohibits segregation or discrimination in places of public accommodation involved in interstate commerce, such as hotels, restaurants, and places of entertainment. Title IV calls for the desegregation of public schools. Title

VII bans discrimination by trade unions, schools, or employers involved in interstate commerce or doing business with the federal government. The latter section also applies to discrimination on the basis of sex and established a government agency, the Equal Employment Opportunity Commission (EEOC), to enforce these provisions.

Reconstruction Renewed

The Civil Rights Act of 1964 is often called the most important U.S. law on civil rights since Reconstruction (1865–77). During the Reconstruction era after the Civil War, the federal government attempted to rectify the injustices of slavery and its political, social, and economic legacy. The most important measures were the Reconstruction amendments: the Thirteenth outlawed slavery; the Fourteenth guaranteed equal protection under the law and due process for all citizens; and the Fifteenth gave black men the right to vote.

But in 1877 the federal government stepped back, removing troops from the former Confederate states and effectively ending its protection of the rights of former slaves. By the turn of the 20th century a new racial system had been put in place in the South: Black voters were disenfranchised, and most public places were segregated. African Americans worked mostly low-wage jobs in agricultural and domestic employment, and there was widespread violence to punish those who challenged the new order.

The Reconstruction amendments were flagrantly violated during this era, but they remained in the Constitution. Charles Sumner, a senator who fought for blacks to have equal voting rights, called them "sleeping giants," to be awakened by future generations who sought to redeem the promise of genuine freedom for the descendants of slavery. Almost one hundred years after the abolition of slavery, the civil rights movement, sometimes called the "second Reconstruction," at last began to fulfill the political and social agenda of Reconstruction. The Civil Rights Act of 1964 was the nation's first major effort in this direction.

The Civil Rights Act was highly controversial. White groups opposed to integration with blacks responded to the act with a significant backlash that took the form of protests, increased support for prosegregation candidates for public office, and some racial violence. The constitutionality of the act was immediately challenged by the Supreme Court case *Heart of Atlanta Motel* v. *U.S.* (1964). The court upheld the act, ruling that its Title II was constitutional.

Along with the Civil Rights Act, Johnson secured passage of his antipoverty bill, the Economic Opportunity Act, in the summer of 1964. This act was an important first step in the war on poverty. It established programs for both youth and adults, such as Head Start, Job Corps, and Adult Basic Education. In his remarks upon signing the bill, Johnson said, "We are not content to accept the endless growth of relief rolls or welfare rolls. We want to offer the forgotten fifth of our people opportunity and not doles."

Landslide Election Victory

After his nomination as the Democratic Party's presidential candidate in 1964,

Johnson's landslide victory in the election of 1964 indicated that he and his reform agenda had widespread support.

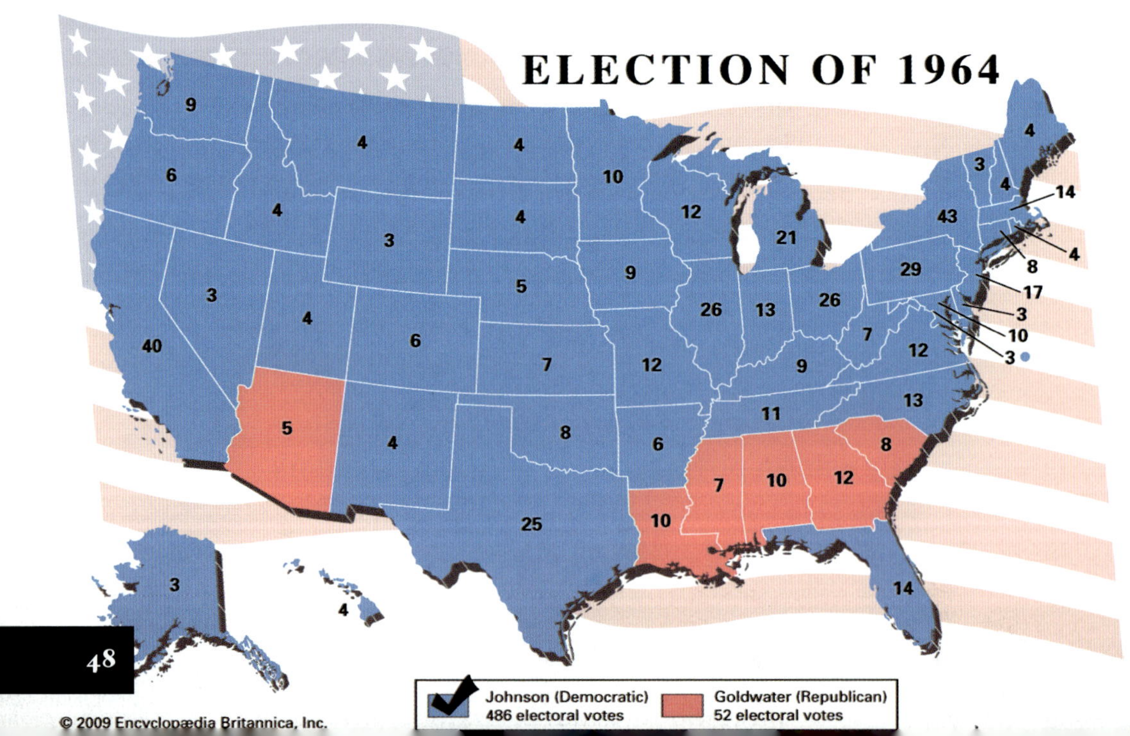

Johnson plunged into the campaign. Attacking the so-called "extremism" of his Republican opponent, Senator Barry M. Goldwater of Arizona, he called for a continuation of bipartisan "peace and prosperity" policies.

In November Johnson was elected president by what was then the greatest landslide in the nation's history. He won 61 percent of the total popular vote and a plurality of nearly 16 million votes. He carried every state except Arizona and five in the Deep South, with 486 electoral college votes. Johnson interpreted his victory as an extraordinary mandate to push forward with his Great Society reforms.

CHAPTER 4

Full Term as President

On January 20, 1965, Johnson was inaugurated for his first full presidential term. In domestic affairs, he expanded his concept of the Great Society. The legislative program proposed by Johnson concentrated on antipoverty, health, education, conservation, and urban planning measures. However, his administration soon faced growing opposition to the ongoing Vietnam War.

The Voting Rights Act

Continuing his commitment to civil rights issues, Johnson pressed Congress for—and obtained—legislation assuring voting rights for blacks. For decades white leaders had used intimidation and fraud to reduce voter registration and turnout among African Americans. In the 1950s and early 1960s Congress enacted laws to protect the right of African Americans to vote, but such legislation was only partially successful. The Civil Rights Act and the Twenty-fourth Amendment were not sufficient to protect voting rights for African Americans. Voter registration rates among African Americans were still well below those of whites.

Johnson with civil rights leaders on the day he signed the Voting Rights Act of 1965. Civil rights activists had pressed the president to support federal legislation with additional protections for black voting rights.

The Voting Rights Act (VRA) of 1965 suspended literacy tests and directed the attorney general of the United States to challenge the use of poll taxes for state and local elections. Sections 4 and 5 of the act provided for oversight of jurisdictions that had previously used tests to determine voter eligibility. If these jurisdictions wanted to change their voting laws or procedures, they would have to obtain federal approval (known as "preclearance") to ensure that the new laws did not disenfranchise black voters.

The VRA resulted in a marked decrease in the voter registration disparity between whites and blacks. In the mid-1960s, for example, the overall proportion of white to black registration in the South ranged from about 2 to 1 to 3 to 1 (and about 10 to 1 in Mississippi). By the late 1980s racial variations in voter registration had largely disappeared. As the number of African American voters increased, so did the number of African American elected officials. In the mid-1960s there were about 70 African American elected officials in the South, but by the turn of the 21st century there were some 5,000, and the number of African American members of Congress had increased from 6 to about 40.

African Americans in Peachtree, Alabama, line up to vote in 1966. Voting rates among blacks began to rise after the Voting Rights Act of 1965.

Sections 4 and 5 of the VRA were extended for 5 years in 1970, 7 years in 1975, and 25 years in both 1982 and 2006. In the 2013 case *Shelby County* v. *Holder*, however, the U.S. Supreme Court struck down Section 4, which had established a formula for identifying jurisdictions that were required to obtain preclearance. The court declared the formula to be unjustified in light of changed historical circumstances.

Congressman John Lewis of Georgia holds a press conference outside the Supreme Court before oral arguments began in *Shelby County* v. *Holder*. A prominent civil rights activist in the 1960s, Lewis had been a leader of the march on Selma, Alabama, which was instrumental in the passage of the Voting Rights Act.

Shelby County v. *Holder* Opinions and Aftermath

The Supreme Court's 5–4 decision in *Shelby County* v. *Holder* on June 25, 2013, was very controversial. The court's opinion was written by Chief Justice John G. Roberts, Jr., and joined by Justices Samuel A. Alito,

Anthony M. Kennedy, Antonin Scalia, and Clarence Thomas, the court's more conservative members. They argued that Section 4 of the VRA was no longer justified now that the gap in voter registration between whites and blacks in the jurisdictions singled out in Section 4 had been almost completely eradicated. The majority recognized that enforcement of the VRA itself had caused the turnaround. Still, they believed that in light of current conditions, it was not right for the federal government to continue monitoring election laws in certain jurisdictions just because those areas had had voting tests or low voter turnout back in the 1960s. The court declared that the formula was an unwarranted intrusion by the federal government on those states' rights to regulate elections, as granted by the Tenth Amendment.

Notably, the court did not find fault with the VRA's Section 5 (which now became unenforceable) or with the notion of preclearance itself. Congress could have designed a new formula for which areas needed to be subject to preclearance, but congressional leaders knew that agreeing on a new formula would have been nearly impossible.

Justice Ruth Bader Ginsburg wrote a dissenting opinion, which was joined by Justices Stephen Breyer, Elena Kagan, and Sonia Sotomayor, the court's more liberal members. Ginsburg read her dissent from the bench as a mark of how strongly she disagreed with the decision. As she put it, "Throwing out preclearance when it has worked and is continuing to work to stop discriminatory changes is like throwing away your umbrella in a rainstorm because you are not getting wet."

The same day that the *Shelby County* decision was announced, the state of Texas declared that its strict voter

continued on the next page

continued from the previous page

identification law would go into effect. This law had been reviewed and rejected by the U.S. Justice Department under Section 5 of the VRA, but now the state did not need federal approval to change its voting requirements. The law was immediately challenged in federal court, and in 2015 a federal appeals court ruled unanimously that it discriminated against black and Latino voters. Proponents of the VRA welcomed the ruling as a sign that the VRA could still protect minorities' voting rights even though the Supreme Court had struck down the preclearance formula.

Domestic Agenda

Johnson won excellent cooperation from the 89th Congress, in which Democrats outnumbered Republicans by a ratio of more than two to one. Legislation passed in July 1965 raised social security payments and taxes. The bill also provided for health benefits for the elderly (Medicare) and low-income Americans (Medicaid).

A $1.3 billion measure to aid public schools and a bill creating a Cabinet-level Department of Housing and Urban Development (HUD) were passed, though similar legislation urged by other presidents had been rejected. Among other things, HUD ensures equal access to housing and community-based employment opportunities, and it carries out programs that serve the housing needs of low-income and minority families and the elderly, the disabled, and the mentally ill. In January 1966 Johnson named as secretary of HUD Robert C. Weaver—the first black to head a Cabinet department. Other major

Johnson (*right*) speaks with Robert C. Weaver, his secretary of housing and urban development (HUD), at the dedication of a new HUD building in 1968.

measures enacted in 1965 included the easing of immigration procedures, a highway beautification act, aid to higher education, and an omnibus housing bill.

The president curtailed his schedule for several weeks after he underwent surgery for removal of his gall bladder in October 1965. His third State of the Union message was delivered in January 1966. He pledged U.S. support in Vietnam "until aggression has stopped" and a continuation of his Great Society programs.

Congress approved many of Johnson's 1966 legislative proposals, including the creation of a Cabinet-level Department of Transportation (DOT). Among the president's proposals rejected by Congress were a civil rights bill with an open-housing provision and constitutional amendments to abolish the electoral college and to lengthen to four years the terms of members of the House of Representatives.

As the United States expanded its participation in the Vietnam War, domestic affairs tended to take a secondary place. Nevertheless, in 1967 the president made many legislative proposals to the first session of the 90th Congress. These included a civil rights bill similar to that rejected in 1966, suggestions for expanding social security and for controlling crime, and a request for an income tax surcharge.

The Twenty-fifth Amendment to the Constitution, ratified in February, settled questions that were unresolved when Johnson succeeded Kennedy. It clarified the role of a vice president in the event of a president's death or disability and that of a president in filling a vice presidential vacancy. Johnson filled Supreme Court vacancies by appointing Abe Fortas in 1965 and Thurgood Marshall, the court's first black justice, in 1967.

Escalation in Vietnam

Despite his campaign pledges not to widen American military involvement in Vietnam, Johnson soon increased the number of U.S. troops in that country and expanded their mission. In February 1965, after an attack by Viet Cong guerrillas on an U.S. military base in Pleiku, Johnson ordered "Operation Rolling Thunder," a series of massive bombing raids on North Vietnam intended to cut supply lines to North Vietnamese and Viet Cong fighters in the

South. He also dispatched 3,500 Marines to protect the border city of Da Nang. Fifty thousand additional troops were sent in July, and by the end of the year the number of military personnel in the country had reached 180,000. The number increased steadily over the next two years, peaking at about 550,000 in 1968.

As each new American escalation met with fresh enemy response and as no end to the combat appeared in sight, the president's public support declined steeply. American casualties gradually mounted, reaching nearly 500 a week by the end of 1967. Moreover, the enormous financial cost of the war, reaching $25 billion in 1967, diverted money from Johnson's cherished Great Society programs and began to fuel inflation.

Beginning in 1965 student demonstrations grew larger and more frequent and helped to stimulate resistance to the draft. From 1967 onward, antiwar sentiment gradually spread among other segments of the population, including liberal Democrats, intellectuals, and civil rights leaders. By 1968 many prominent political figures, some of them former supporters of the president's Vietnam policies, were publicly calling for an early negotiated settlement of the war.

Soldiers lead a protest against the Vietnam War in New York City.

As his popularity sank to new lows in 1967, Johnson was confronted by demonstrations almost everywhere he went. It pained him to hear protesters, especially students—whom he thought would respect him for his progressive social agenda—chanting, "Hey, hey, LBJ, how many kids did you kill today?" To avoid the demonstrations, he eventually restricted his travels, becoming a virtual "prisoner" in the White House.

Race Riots

Meanwhile, life for the nation's poor, particularly African Americans living in inner-city slums in the North, failed to show significant improvement. Vast numbers of African Americans still suffered from unemployment, run-down schools, and lack of adequate medical care, and many were malnourished or hungry. Expectations of prosperity arising from the promise of the Great Society failed to materialize. Discontent and alienation

The aftermath of race riots in Detroit in 1967

grew accordingly, fed in part by a surge in African American political radicalism and calls for black power.

Beginning in the mid-1960s violence erupted in several cities as the country suffered through "long, hot summers" of riots or the threat of riots in the Watts district of Los Angeles (1965), Cleveland, Ohio (1966), Newark, New Jersey, and Detroit, Michigan (1967), Washington, D.C. (1968), and elsewhere. Fears of a general "race war" were in the air. The president responded by appointing a special panel to report on the crisis, the National Advisory Commission on Civil Disorders. The commission concluded that the country was in danger of dividing into two societies—one white, one black, "separate and unequal."

More Trouble Abroad

On January 23, 1968, an American intelligence-gathering vessel, the USS *Pueblo*, was seized by North Korea; all 80 members of the crew were captured and imprisoned. Already frustrated by the demands of the Vietnam War, Johnson responded with restraint but called up 15,000 navy and air force reservists and ordered the nuclear-powered aircraft carrier USS *Enterprise* to the area. The *Pueblo* crew was held for 11 months and was freed only after the United States apologized for having violated North Korean waters; the apology was later retracted.

To make matters worse, only one week after the seizure of the *Pueblo*, the Tet Offensive by North Vietnamese and Viet

U.S. military policemen help an injured colleague at the U.S. Embassy in Saigon on January 31, 1961, early in the Tet Offensive.

Cong forces in South Vietnam embarrassed the Johnson Administration and shocked the country. Although the attack was a failure in military terms, the news coverage—including televised images of enemy forces firing on the U.S. embassy in Saigon, the South Vietnamese capital—completely undermined the administration's claim that the war was being won and added further to Johnson's nagging "credibility gap."

Johnson Decides Not to Run

Meanwhile, Senator Eugene McCarthy declared his candidacy for the Democratic presidential nomination, an unprecedented affront to a sitting president. Robert Kennedy, former attorney general and brother of the late John F. Kennedy, announced his own candidacy soon thereafter. On March 31, 1968, Johnson startled television viewers with a national address that included three announcements: that he had just ordered major reductions in the bombing of North Vietnam, that he was requesting peace talks, and that he would neither seek nor accept his party's renomination for the presidency.

Johnson prepares to deliver the March 31, 1968, speech in which he announced his decision not to run for reelection.

In the last year of his presidency Johnson traveled to El Salvador, where he discussed Central American economic integration with the presidents of El Salvador, Costa Rica, Honduras, Nicaragua, and Guatemala. He also proposed a nuclear nonproliferation treaty in an effort to improve relations between the United States and the Soviet Union. However, he condemned the Soviet-led invasion of Czechoslovakia in August 1968, and his hopes to visit the Soviet Union were foiled.

The assassination of African American civil rights leader Martin Luther King, Jr., in April 1968 provoked new rioting in Washington, D.C., and elsewhere. Two months later Robert Kennedy was shot dead in Los Angeles, and the Democratic presidential nomination of Vice President Hubert Humphrey was ensured.

Meanwhile, negotiations had begun with the North Vietnamese. In October, one week before the election, Johnson announced an end to the bombing in North Vietnam, to be followed by direct negotiations with Hanoi. But it was too late for Humphrey, who narrowly lost the election to the Republican candidate, Richard Nixon, by a popular vote of nearly 30.9 million to Nixon's 31.7 million.

Conclusion

Johnson was succeeded by Nixon on January 20, 1969. He then retired to his Texas ranch. There he wrote *The Vantage Point* (1971) and helped establish both a library to house his presidential papers and the Lyndon Baines Johnson School of Public Affairs at the University of Texas in Austin.

On January 22, 1973, Johnson suffered a fatal heart attack at his ranch, just a few days before the end of the war in Vietnam. Later in 1973, the space center at Houston was

The mission control room at the Johnson Space Center during a spacewalk in 2013

renamed the Lyndon Baines Johnson Space Center in his memory.

When he left office, Johnson remarked, "I hope it may be said, 100 years from now, that we helped to make this country more just. That's what I hope. But I believe that at least it will be said that we tried." The social programs he enacted—from Head Start to Medicare—transformed American society, but his decision to increase the U.S. role in Vietnam hampered his efforts to build on the extraordinary legislative achievements of his first two years in office. Subsequent administrations struggled to fund these programs and to find support for additional reforms on issues such as welfare and health care. Though President Johnson's goals of economic and social equality for all Americans remain unfulfilled, the progress made during his five years in office is undeniable.

Glossary

affront An action or statement that insults or offends someone.

alienation A withdrawing or separation of a person or a person's affections from an object or position of former attachment.

bipartisanship Formulation of government policy by compromise and agreement between two major political parties.

cloture The closing or limitation of debate in a legislative body by calling for a vote or by other authorized methods.

conservative Relating to a political party or point of view that advocates preservation of established and traditional practices.

continuity Uninterrupted connection, succession, or union.

credibility gap A lack of trust or believability.

faction A group within a larger group that has different ideas and opinions than the rest of the group.

forebear Ancestor.

guerrilla A member of a group of soldiers who do not belong to a government's military forces and who wage fast-moving, small-scale actions against conventional forces.

inflation A continuing rise in the general price level usually attributed to an increase in the volume of money and credit relative to available goods.

institutionalize To incorporate into a system of organized belief or practice.

ironic Using words that mean the opposite of the literal sense of the words.

liberal Relating to a political party or point of view that advocates social and political change.

mandate Approval given by voters to their elected representative.

nonproliferation Providing for the stoppage of production, especially of nuclear weapons.

omnibus bill A legislative bill that combines a number of separate measures.

poll tax A tax of a fixed amount per person, payment of which is often made a requirement for voting.

preclearance Formal authorization in advance.

scion Descendant especially of a wealthy, aristocratic, or influential family.

tantamount Equal in value, significance, or effect.

trustee A person who has been given responsibility for managing someone else's property or money.

urbanity The quality or state of being confident and polished in manner.

For More Information

LBJ Presidential Library
2313 Red River Street
Austin, TX 78705
(512) 721-0200
Website: http://www.lbjlibrary.org
In addition to the exhibits and events at its physical location, the LBJ Presidential Library has online exhibits on such topics as civil rights, Johnson's correspondence with his wife, Lady Bird, and the transition to Johnson's presidency after Kennedy's assassination.

The Miller Center
P.O. Box 400406
Charlottesville, VA 22904
(434) 924-7236
Website: http://millercenter.org
The Miller Center, based at the University of Virginia, is a nonpartisan research

facility focused on the history of the U.S. presidency. One of the center's ongoing projects is to transcribe and interpret the secret White House recordings of presidents Franklin D. Roosevelt, Harry S. Truman, Dwight D. Eisenhower, John F. Kennedy, Lyndon B. Johnson, and Richard Nixon.

NASA's Lyndon B. Johnson Space Center
2101 NASA Parkway
Houston, TX 77058
(281) 483-0123
Website: http://www.nasa.gov/centers/johnson/home/index.html
NASA's Manned Spaceflight Center in Houston, Texas, was renamed in honor of Lyndon B. Johnson in 1973. It was the headquarters for the early space programs Gemini, Apollo, and Skylab. It is the home of mission control for all NASA missions and International Space Center operations.

National Association for the Advancement of Colored People (NAACP)
4805 Mt. Hope Drive
Baltimore, MD 21215
(410) 580-5777

Website: http://www.naacp.org
Founded in 1909, the NAACP aims to eliminate discrimination and achieve equality between people of all races. Its members were among the leaders of the civil rights movement of the 1950s and 1960s.

U.S. Department of Housing and Urban Development (HUD)
451 7th Street SW
Washington, DC 20410
(202) 708-1112
Website: http://portal.hud.gov/hudportal/HUD
HUD became a cabinet-level department of the federal government in 1965. It focuses on providing quality affordable housing and creating inclusive communities.

Websites

Because of the changing nature of Internet links, Rosen Educational Services has developed an online list of websites related to the subject of this book. This site is updated regularly. Please use this link to access the list:

http://www.rosenlinks.com/PPPL/lbj

For Further Reading

Berman, Ari. *Give Us the Ballot: The Modern Struggle for Voting Rights in America.* New York, NY: Farrar, Straus and Giroux, 2015.

Bringle, Jennifer. *The Civil Rights Act of 1964* (A Celebration of the Civil Rights Movement). New York, NY: Rosen Publishing, 2015.

Feinstein, Stephen. *The 1960s* (Decades of the 20th and 21st Centuries). New York, NY: Enslow Publishing, 2015.

Kaufman, Michael T. *1968*. New York, NY: Roaring Brook Press, 2009.

Kent, Deborah. *The Vietnam War: From Da Nang to Saigon* (The United States at War). Berkeley Heights, NJ: Enslow Publishers, 2011.

Killcoyne, Hope Lourie, ed. *The Civil Rights Era* (The African American Experience). New York, NY: Britannica Educational Publishing, 2016.

Killcoyne, Hope Lourie, ed. *Key Figures of the Vietnam War* (Biographies of War). New York, NY: Britannica Educational Publishing, 2016.

May, Gary. *Bending Toward Justice: The Voting Rights Act and the Transformation of American Democracy*. New York, NY: Basic Books, 2013.

Pach, Chester. *The Johnson Years* (Presidential Profiles). New York, NY: Facts on File, 2005.

Reid, Scott. *The Great Society* (Perspectives on Modern World History). Farmington Hills, MI: Greenhaven Press, 2015.

Risen, Clay. *The Bill of the Century: The Epic Battle for the Civil Rights Act*. New York, NY: Bloomsbury Press, 2014.

Samuels, Charlie. *The Tet Offensive* (Turning Points in US Military History). New York, NY: Gareth Stevens Publishing, 2014.

Swanson, James L. *"The President Has Been Shot!": The Assassination of John F. Kennedy*. New York, NY: Scholastic Press, 2013.

Zelizer, Julian E. *The Fierce Urgency of Now: Lyndon Johnson, Congress, and the Battle for the Great Society*. New York, NY: Penguin Books, 2015.

Index

H

I

J

K

L

M

N